YANG THE YOUNGEST AND HIS TERRIBLE EAR

by
Lensey Namioka

Teacher Guide

Written by
Elizabeth M. Klar and
Cheryl Klar-Trim

Edited by
Katherine E. Martinez

Note

The Yearling paperback edition of the book, published by Bantam Doubleday Dell Books for Young Readers ©1992, was used to prepare this guide. The page references may differ in other editions.

Please note: Please assess the appropriateness of this book for the age level and maturity of your students prior to reading and discussing it with your class.

To order, contact your local school
supply store, or—

Copyright 2002 by Novel Units, Inc., San Antonio, Texas. All rights reserved. No part of this publication may be reproduced, stored in a retrieval system, or transmitted in [...] photocopying, recording, or otherwise) without prior writ[...] following exceptions: Photocopying of student worksheets [...] his/her own class is permissible. Reproduction of any part of [...] system or for commercial sale is strictly prohibited. **Copyrigh**[...]

Novel Units is a registered trademark of Novel Units, Inc.

Printed in the United States of America.

PAPERBACKS - BMI BOUND BOOKS
TEACHER'S GUIDES - AUDIO-VISUALS
PO BOX 800 - DAYTON, N.J. 08810-0800
Toll Free Phone 1-800-222-8100
America's Finest Educational Book Distributor

www.bmionline.com

Table of Contents

Skills and Strategies

Thinking
Identifying attributes, research, compare/contrast, pros/cons, brainstorming, problem solving, creative thinking, patterns, critical thinking

Comprehension
Predictions, conflict, sequencing, cause and effect, inference

Listening/Speaking
Dramatizing, interviewing, storytelling, discussion, oral reports, music

Literary Elements
Literary analysis, story mapping, characterization

Vocabulary
Charades, word maps, synonyms, antonyms, defining, parts of speech, context clues

Across the Curriculum
Social Studies—culture, law, immigration; Art—drawing, design and color, diorama, collage, puppet making, advertisements, comic strip; Technology—Web page, Internet; Sports—history, rules; Drama—reenactments

Writing
Character journal, poetry, letters, personal writing, review, creative writing, titles, diary

Summary

Yang the Youngest and His Terrible Ear tells the story of Yingtao, a nine-year-old Chinese immigrant, who does not excel on the violin. His father wants all four of his children to become accomplished musicians, but Yingtao is tone-deaf and cannot play on key. While trying to make new friends at school, Yingtao meets Matthew, who introduces him to the game of baseball. Matthew loves to play the violin, but his father wants him to be a great baseball player. The two friends think up a plan to help each other win their fathers' praise and still fulfill their own dreams.

About the Author

Lensey Namioka has written numerous books for children. Many of her humorous books deal with a variety of social and cultural issues that affect the four children of the Yang family. Lensey Namioka currently resides in Seattle, Washington.

Introductory Activities

1. Previewing the Book: Have students look at the cover and answer the journalist's questions about what they see: Who? What? When? Where? and Why? Based on their answers, students predict what the book will be about.

2. Predicting: Given the following clues, students write a paragraph predicting what they think will happen in the story.

   recital   dedication   Chinese   practice   baseball   music

3. Character Journal: List the main characters from *Yang the Youngest and His Terrible Ear* and have students choose one. As they read the book, students should write regular entries from that character's point of view. Journal entries should reflect on the events of the story. At various points in their reading, have students share their journals with classmates.

4. Attribute Web: Create an attribute web (see page 10 of this guide) with students for each of the following ideas: friends, tone-deaf, practice, obedience, and baseball. Ask students to quickly tell what each word brings to mind. Encourage students to elaborate on particular ideas.

5. Prediction Chart: Have students set up a prediction chart (see pages 6-7 of this guide) to use as they read the book.

6. Anticipation Questions: Have students respond to each of the following statements with a "thumbs up" (I agree) or a "thumbs down" (I disagree) and discuss their responses.

   • Children should always follow their parents' wishes.
   • You should not tease people who have different customs or ideas.
   • Friends should help and support each other.

- Parents should always encourage their children's interests and hobbies.
- Parents love their children equally.
- Most people have hidden talents and abilities.
- Practice makes perfect.
- People who play an instrument are smarter than people who play a sport.

Vocabulary Activities

1. Target Word Charades: Have students act out some of the vocabulary words and have classmates guess the target word. Some suggested words for *Yang the Youngest and His Terrible Ear*:

   muttered (14)   snigger (19)   annoyed (58)   glaring (62)
   lip sync (71)   scaling (88)   kneaded (107)   winced (123)

2. Target Word Maps: Have students complete word maps for vocabulary words of a certain part of speech. For example, adjectives from *Yang the Youngest and His Terrible Ear* would include:

   dedicated (13)   sympathetic (36)   scrawny (39)   brilliant (70)
   dazzling (110)   dazed (117)

Word Map for an Adjective

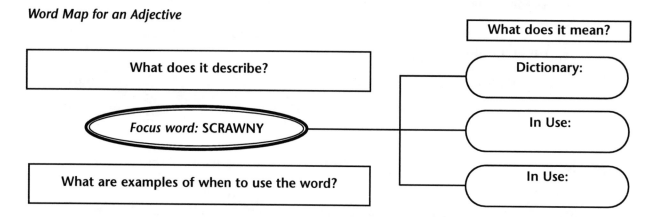

3. Sentences: Have students select five or six vocabulary words and use as many of the words as possible in one sentence.

4. Synonym Match: Have students select vocabulary words from a chapter and list one synonym for each vocabulary word on a small piece of paper. Students mix the pieces of paper and match each synonym to the appropriate vocabulary word.

5. Catch a Carp Game: Cut carp patterns from construction paper. The fish patterns should be large enough to fit a vocabulary word. Glue a piece of magnetic tape on the back of each fish. Place all of the fish on a sheet of blue poster board. Construct a fishing pole from a dowel or ruler by attaching a string to one end of the pole and a magnet to the end of the

string. Each student takes a turn fishing for a vocabulary word. When a fish is caught, the student must give the definition of the word or use the word in a sentence. If the student is correct, he/she gets to keep the fish. If the student is incorrect he/she must throw the fish back into the water. A variation of the game would be to write the definition on the fish and instruct the students to say the vocabulary word. The person or team who catches the most fish wins the game.

6. Vocabulary Sort: Have the students sort vocabulary words into categories (e.g., nouns, verbs, and adjectives/adverbs).

7. Odd One Out: Use vocabulary words from one or two chapters. Have the students make a chain of four words. One word in the chain is the vocabulary word, two words are synonyms for the vocabulary word, and one word does not go with the others. (Mix the sequence of the words in the chain.) Students should exchange their chains with classmates, underline the word that does not belong with the others, and explain why it does not belong.

8. Vocabulary Boxes: Cut a pattern for a cube (pattern below) from construction paper. Before the cube is glued together, each face should contain one of the following: a vocabulary word, the definition of the word, an illustration of the word, a synonym of the word, an antonym of the word, and a sentence using the word. Display the vocabulary boxes in the room.

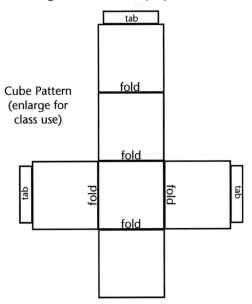

Cube Pattern
(enlarge for
class use)

9. Baseball Match: Have students cut large baseballs from construction paper. The students should write a vocabulary word on one side of each ball, and glue a piece of Velcro on the other. Cover the bulletin board with a piece of felt that has the outline of a baseball field (three bases and home plate) on it. Label first base "Say It," second base "Define It," third base "Use It" (in a sentence), and home plate "Replace It" (with a synonym). Divide students into teams of nine. Each student, in turn, selects a ball and takes that word through the bases. Completing all four bases in one turn equals a "home run" and scores three points for the team. If the student scores only a base hit, the ball stays on the board until a teammate completes the bases and scores one point for the team. Each student gets one turn per "inning." Play continues until all words are used .

Using Predictions

We all make predictions as we read—little guesses about what will happen next, how a conflict will be resolved, which details will be important to the plot, which details will help fill in our sense of a character. Students should be encouraged to predict, to make sensible guesses as they read the novel.

As students work on their predictions, these discussion questions can be used to guide them: What are some of the ways to predict? What is the process of a sophisticated reader's thinking and predicting? What clues does an author give to help us make predictions? Why are some predictions more likely to be accurate than others?

Create a chart for recording predictions. This could be either an individual or class activity. As each subsequent chapter is discussed, students can review and correct their previous predictions about plot and characters as necessary.

Use the facts and ideas the author gives.

Use your own prior knowledge.

Apply any new information (i.e., from class discussion) that may cause you to change your mind.

Predictions

_____

_____

_____

_____

_____

Prediction Chart

What characters have we met so far?	What is the conflict in the story?	What are your predictions?	Why did you make those predictions?

© Novel Units, Inc.

Using Character Webs

Attribute webs are simply a visual representation of a character from the novel. They provide a systematic way for students to organize and recap the information they have about a particular character. Attribute webs may be used after reading the novel to recapitulate information about a particular character, or completed gradually as information unfolds. They may be completed individually or as a group project.

One type of character attribute web uses these divisions:

- How a character acts and feels. (How does the character act? How do you think the character feels? How would you feel if this happened to you?)

- How a character looks. (Close your eyes and picture the character. Describe him/her to me.)

- Where a character lives. (Where and when does the character live?)

- How others feel about the character. (How does another specific character feel about our character?)

In group discussion about the characters described in student attribute webs, the teacher can ask for backup proof from the novel. Inferential thinking can be included in the discussion.

Attribute webs need not be confined to characters. They may also be used to organize information about a concept, object, or place.

Attribute Web

The attribute web below will help you gather clues the author provides about a character in the novel. Fill in the blanks with words and phrases which tell how the character acts and looks, as well as what the character says and what others say about him or her.

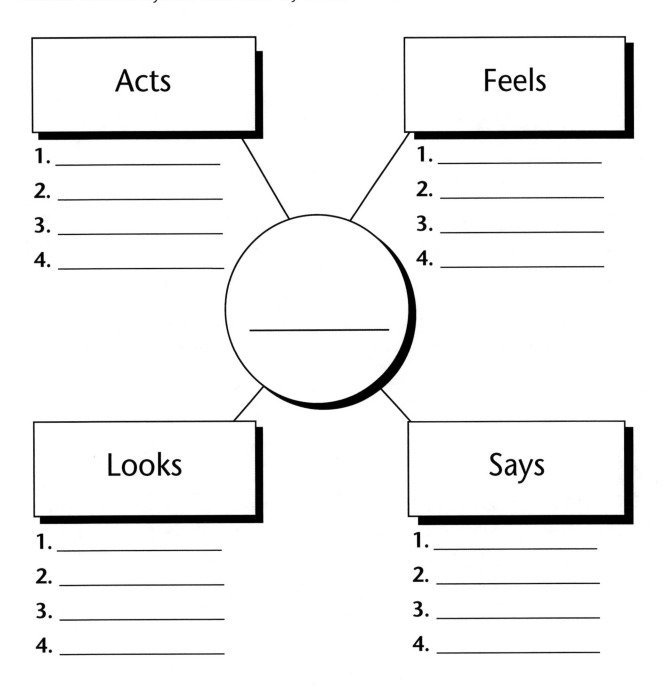

Acts

1. _____
2. _____
3. _____
4. _____

Feels

1. _____
2. _____
3. _____
4. _____

Looks

1. _____
2. _____
3. _____
4. _____

Says

1. _____
2. _____
3. _____
4. _____

Attribute Web

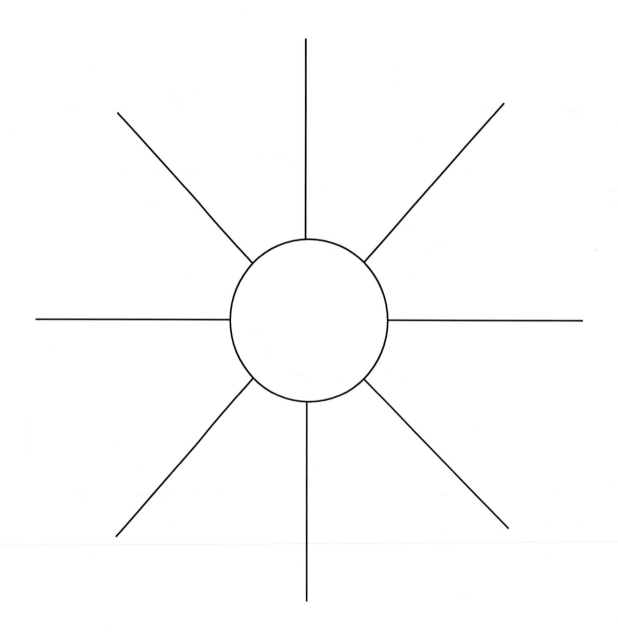

Story Map

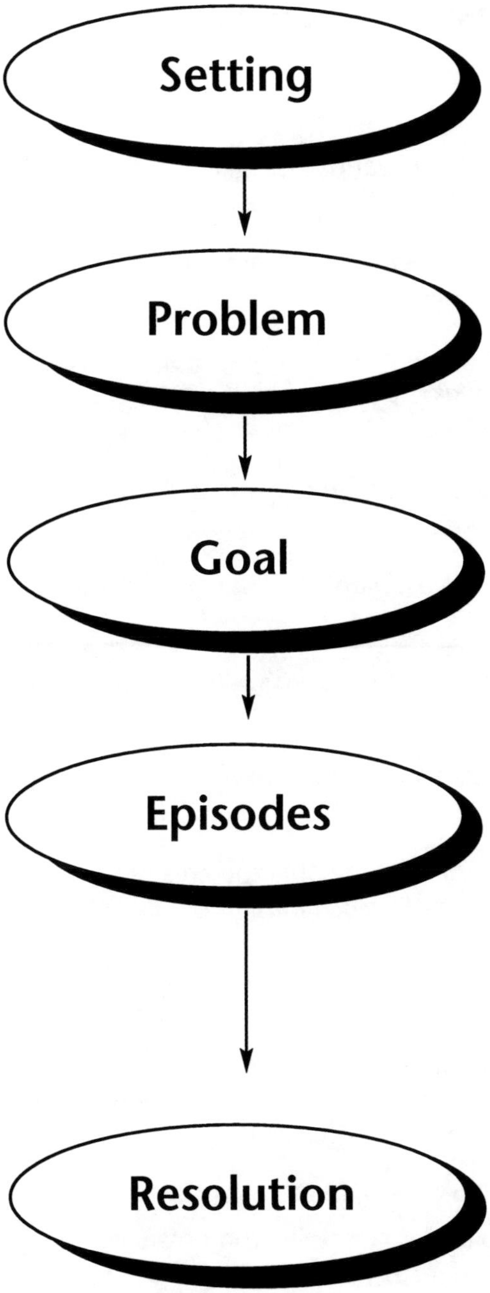

Characters_____

_____

Time and Place_____

_____

Problem_____

_____

_____

Goal_____

_____

_____

Beginning ——→ Development ——→ Outcome

_____

_____

_____

_____

Resolution_____

_____

_____

_____

Setting

Problem

Goal

Episodes

Resolution

Chapter 1

Vocabulary

bow (3)	viola (3)	cello (3)	elder (3)
alternate (6)	pitch (7)	mutant (10)	mute (10)
impression (11)	dedicated (13)	muttered (14)	wallowing (15)
anxious (15)			

Discussion Questions

1. Why doesn't Yingtao call his oldest brother and sister by their real names? *(He is not allowed to because of a Chinese custom.)*

2. Why is Yingtao's father able to find a job with the symphony while his mother is not? *(The symphony only needs one pianist but has room for several violinists.)*

3. How is Yingtao's father able to communicate with his students even though he speaks very little English? *(He smiles when the students play well and makes a face when they play sour notes.)*

4. Why does Yingtao feel closest to Third Sister? *(She is closest to him in age and is the only one who seems to understand that he is really trying his best with his music.)*

5. What does Yingtao mean when he says he is tone-deaf? *(He is unable to distinguish differences in pitch, high or low sounds, in music.)*

6. How does Eldest Brother's personality differ from the rest of the children's? *(He is more serious than the rest of them and does not like to waste time.)*

7. Why is the recital so important to Yingtao's family? *(If the students and the Yang children play well, then the students' parents will spread the word and Mr. Yang will get more students.)*

8. Why is Yingtao worried about playing in the recital? *(He thinks if the other parents see how poorly he plays they won't have confidence in Mr. Yang's ability to teach music.)*

9. Why can't Yingtao get a good grip on his bow as he practices for the recital? *(He is so nervous that his hands are sweating and the bow keeps slipping.)*

10. How does Yingtao know that his parents love him? *(He remembers how relieved his father looked after he saw that all four children were safely strapped into their seats on the plane from Shanghai and the way his mother divided the Hershey bar into four equal pieces.)*

Supplementary Activities

1. Art/Research: Have students use the Internet to obtain pictures of the instruments used in a string quartet. Ask several students to draw pictures of the instruments and label them. Display in the classroom.

2. Music: Obtain a recording of a string quartet to play during class.

3. Music: Have students act out and sing the song "Old McDonald Had a Farm" or play a recording and have students point out the key changes and different tones.

4. Writing/Critical Thinking: Have students pretend they are Yingtao and write a paragraph describing how they feel about practicing the violin. Students may draw a picture of Yingtao to go along with their paragraphs.

Chapter 2

Vocabulary

snigger (19)	wistfully (21)	lamely (22)	audition (23)
trombone (24)	moody (27)	apologetically (35)	sympathetic (36)

Discussion Questions

1. Why does Yingtao experience difficulty making friends when he first arrives in America? *(He cannot speak English, he arrives in the middle of the school year so the other students already know each other, and the behavior of the American children scares him.)*

2. How is Third Sister a help to Yingtao during his first days at school? *(She keeps him company at school.)*

3. What makes Yingtao believe that Second Sister is the loneliest? *(In China, everyone always told her how beautiful she was and she had many friends. In America, not many people tell her she is pretty.)*

4. Why does Yingtao's teacher seat him next to a Korean girl? Why doesn't sitting next to the Korean girl help Yingtao feel more comfortable? *(They are both Asian Americans; The Korean girl does not speak Chinese. She is just as much a stranger to Yingtao as the other children.)*

5. How do you think Yingtao feels when Jake takes his pen and he tries to explain to the teacher what happened? *(Answers will vary.)*

6. Why is Yingtao tempted to agree to play the triangle? *(Yingtao has good timing, which is all one needs in order to play the triangle.)*

7. Why does Matthew seem embarrassed when Yingtao asks if he wants to take violin lessons? *(Matthew's parents cannot afford lessons.)*

8. Why does Third Sister tell Matthew she is a terrible cellist? *(That is the way her parents taught her to respond when someone gives her a compliment.)*

9. Why do you think Matthew is confused about Second Sister cutting up tea bags? *(Answers will vary.)*

10. Why is Matthew shocked to learn that the live carp are for dinner? *(This is one of the cultural differences between Matthew's family and the Yang family. Matthew is used to eating fish sticks or canned fish.)*

11. Why does Matthew just stare at his food while the rest of the family eats? What is wrong? *(Matthew has never eaten with chopsticks and does not know how to use them.)*

12. Why does Second Sister disagree with Matthew when he remarks that using chopsticks will help him play the violin better? *(Yingtao has been using chopsticks since he was two years old and still cannot play well.)*

13. Do you think Matthew will be a good friend to Yingtao? Use the book to support your answer. *(Answers will vary.)*

Supplementary Activities

1. Research: Have students research ways to travel to America. Ask a student to write a letter to the Department of Immigration and Naturalization office asking for the rules for immigrating to America. Students should present their findings to the class.

2. Critical Thinking: Use a T-chart to compare and contrast the Chinese student customs of showing respect to a teacher with the American customs of respect. Accept all reasonable student responses.

3. Writing: Ask students to bring a pair of chopsticks to school or provide a set for each class member. Provide finger food for the students or ask them to eat their lunch using only the chopsticks. Students should use their experience to detail the pros and cons of using chopsticks. Instruct them to write an essay on their experience.

Chapter 3

rickshaw (46) *embarrassing (49)* *(52)*
cooperate (46) *fond (45)*

Vocabulary

drilled (38)	slouch (38)	admiration (38)	scrawny (39)
furiously (42)	mumbled (45)	rickshaw (46)	persimmon (50)

good impression (53)

Discussion Questions

1. How do Matthew and Yingtao help each other in school? *(Yingtao helps Matthew with math and Matthew helps Yingtao with spelling.)*

2. Why do the kids at school think Yingtao is a math genius? Why doesn't he tell them the truth? *(Chinese schools are ahead of American schools in math so Yingtao always finishes his math work first; He likes having the other students believe he is good at something.)*

3. Why does Matthew think Yingtao is tough? How does this make Yingtao feel? *(Yingtao is not bothered when the other children make fun of him; He feels twice as tall.)*

4. Why does Yingtao find the game of baseball confusing the first time he plays? *(He does not understand the rules of the game. The terminology is unfamiliar to him; words like "bat," "ball," and "strike" seem to have different meanings than what he has already learned in English.)*

5. How does playing baseball make Yingtao feel? *(He is happy to do something that makes people smile; their approval gives him a happy, floating-away feeling.)*

6. Why does Yingtao feel a little guilty about practicing baseball after school? *(He knows he should spend that time practicing the violin.)*

7. How does Mr. Yang react when Yingtao tells him he has been playing baseball? *(He looks sad and begs Yingtao to try harder when playing the violin.)*

8. What is Mr. Yang's reason for having the children play as a quartet instead of having Eldest Brother play a solo? *(In a solo, one cares only about one's self. In a quartet, one must cooperate with the others while still speaking out for one's self.)*

9. How does Mr. Yang differ from other Chinese fathers? *(In most Chinese families, the father makes all the decisions. In the Yang family, Mr. Yang encourages everyone to speak out and lets each voice be heard.)*

10. Why doesn't Matthew move to a different spot near the better violin players after he improves? *(The teacher is too busy to notice that Matthew has improved. Matthew will have to wait for the next round of auditions to be evaluated.)*

11. What makes Yingtao realize that being his friend could be embarrassing for Matthew? *(Jake sees Matthew and Yingtao on the bus with a fifty-pound bag of rice and makes fun of Matthew.)*

12. How does Yingtao feel as he watches Matthew play in the quartet with his siblings? *(He feels left out.)*

13. Why doesn't Mrs. Conner want Matthew spending so much time at the Yang house? *(She is embarrassed that he is eating dinner there so often.)*

14. Why do you think Mrs. Conner invites Yingtao to dinner at her house? Why do you think Yingtao wants to make a good impression? *(Answers will vary.)*

Supplementary Activities

1. Sports: Ask interested students to research the basic rules of baseball. Students who do the research should prepare a short essay and present their findings to the class.

2. Art: Have students draw a picture of Matthew playing his violin in the string quartet as Yingtao looks on.

3. Writing/Poetry: Have students recall a time someone teased or made fun of them. Students should write a poem about their experience.

Chapter 4

Vocabulary

startled (54)	executives (55)	tuxedo (58)	annoyed (58)
machinist (58)	unemployment (59)	benefits (59)	casserole (62)
glaring (62)	hunch (63)	nerd (68)	brilliant (70)

Discussion Questions

1. Why is Yingtao surprised to learn that Mrs. Conner drives a car? *(He thought the Conners would be too poor to afford a car. In China, only the officials and executives of big companies had cars.)*

2. Why does Matthew think that the Yang family must not be too poor? *(They have expensive instruments.)*

3. Why does Matthew have to get up early in the morning? *(He has a paper route.)*

4. How does Matthew react when Yingtao doesn't understand what "baby-sitting" means? *(He tugs at his hair and takes deep breaths.)*

5. Why doesn't Yingtao have any spare time to get a job? *(When he is not in school he is studying or practicing music.)*

6. How does Yingtao's reaction to Mrs. Conner's meal differ from Eric's reaction? *(Matthew's brother complains about the meal, but Yingtao likes it.)*

7. How does Yingtao feel when Matthew accuses Eric of never listening? *(He is glad the comment is being directed at someone else.)*

8. What did Mrs. Yang do to help her children learn how to eat like Americans? *(She gave them lessons and bought them a book on etiquette.)*

9. Why do you think Yingtao tells the Conners that he enjoyed doing gymnastics when he lived in China? *(Answers will vary.)*

10. Why doesn't Yingtao help Mrs. Conner with the dinner dishes? *(Eric stops him from helping and tells Yingtao that guests don't have to help with the dishes.)*

11. Why do you think Eric is upset about Matthew playing the violin? *(Answers will vary.)*

12. Explain why Matthew and Yingtao think it would be good to trade places. *(Matthew lives with a family that does not appreciate his music and wishes he would stop playing. Yingtao's family doesn't like the way he plays the violin, but does like the way Matthew plays. Yingtao wishes he could stop playing the violin.)*

Supplementary Activities

1. Critical Thinking: As a class, use a T-chart to compare and contrast the differences between Yingtao's family and Matthew's family. Have students write a short paragraph explaining which family is more like their own.

2. Culture: The Yang children read a book on etiquette to help them learn American customs. Have students research the proper etiquette to use at the dinner table. Bring a place setting of dishes to school and have the students practice setting a proper table. After preparing a proper place setting, have each student share at least three rules of good manners that should be followed while dining.

3. Creative Writing: Matthew and Yingtao think it would be nice to trade places. Instruct students to think about someone, real or imaginary, with whom they would like to trade places. Students should write a short story describing what it would be like to trade places with this person.

Chapter 5

Vocabulary

lip sync (71)	sniffed (73)	depression (75)	homesick (76)
console (76)	canals (76)	snuffles (77)	professionally (78)
keen (78)	mythical (79)	definite (79)	concentrating (81)
guinea pigs (85)	scaling (88)	accurately (89)	brooding (91)
impressed (91)	jeered (91)	channeling (92)	frittering (93)

Discussion Questions

1. How does Yingtao plan to solve his problem about playing in the recital? *(He wants to "bow sync" by having Matthew stand behind a screen during the recital while Yingtao pretends to play.)*

2. How does Yingtao know that Matthew is a real music lover? *(Matthew doesn't play the violin to impress anyone. He plays because he enjoys it.)*

3. What do you think Third Sister means when she tells Yingtao, "You can't make a silk purse out of a sow's ear" (p. 74)? *(She means that they can't make a tone-deaf person, or a sow's ear, into a violinist, or silk purse.)*

4. How does Third Sister convince the rest of the family to use the screen during the recital? *(She offers to paint a pair of Chinese scenes on the folding screen. This gets Second Sister interested in helping and their mother is pleased.)*

5. Why do you think Second Sister cries as she paints the scenes on the screen? *(Answers will vary.)*

6. How do you think Yingtao feels when he notices that the people watching him as he goes to bat are looking at him hopefully instead of cringing? *(Answers will vary.)*

7. How does Mr. Conner's accusing Matthew of not paying attention during the baseball game remind Yingtao of his own father? *(Yingtao's father usually tells Yingtao that he is not a better violinist because he is not trying hard enough or not concentrating.)*

8. Why does Yingtao fear that he might never play baseball again? *(Mr. Yang tells Yingtao that he cannot play baseball again until his violin playing improves.)*

9. Why is Matthew so tired that he keeps striking out at bat? *(Between baseball practice, violin practice, schoolwork, and his paper route he is too tired to pay attention.)*

10. How do you think Mrs. Yang feels when the ladies in the grocery store criticize her for taking the broccoli leaves? Why do you think they made fun of her? *(Answers will vary.)*

11. How do Mr. and Mrs. Yang first react to the idea of their children working to earn extra money? *(Mrs. Yang doesn't think that anyone will want to pay the girls to baby-sit. Mr. Yang doesn't think that his children should sacrifice their study and practice time in order to make money.)*

Supplementary Activities

1. Sports/History: Ask an interested student to research the life of Babe Ruth and answer the following questions: What is his real name? What are some of his accomplishments? What are some of his nicknames? The student should write a short report detailing his/her findings.

2. Music/History: Ask a student to research the life of Isaac Stern and answer the following questions: What instrument(s) does Isaac Stern play? What are some of his accomplishments? The student should write a short report detailing his/her findings.

3. Law: In groups of three or four students, research labor laws to determine at what age a child can begin working. What are the current age minimums, wage minimums, and hourly stipulations? What money is deducted from a worker's paycheck? Each group should work together on a report or presentation and share their findings with the class.

4. Literary Analysis: Explain that foreshadowing is the literary technique of giving clues to coming events in a story. The author, Lensey Namioka, uses foreshadowing at the end of Chapter 5 when she writes, "...my parents did something that would make it quite impossible for Matthew to play." Have students write a short paragraph predicting what they think will happen next.

Chapter 6

Vocabulary

beaming (97)	Cantonese (99)	Shanghai (99)	trembled (100)
reluctantly (103)	suspicious (103)	clarinet (105)	kneaded (107)
dabbed (107)	sync (108)	swishing (110)	dazzling (110)
sheepishly (112)			

Discussion Questions

1. Why doesn't Matthew come for his lessons anymore? *(His father gets mad at him because he is spending too much time playing music and not enough time practicing baseball.)*

2. Why are Mr. and Mrs. Yang shocked to hear that Matthew's father is upset? *(They can't imagine anyone scolding a son for practicing his music too much.)*

3. Why doesn't Yingtao want the Conner family to come to the recital? *(If the family comes, Matthew will be sitting in the audience and not behind the screen taking Yingtao's place.)*

4. According to Mrs. Yang, how will Matthew's presence at the recital help Yingtao? *(Matthew will help Yingtao's morale.)*

5. Why do Yingtao and Third Sister stop arguing with their parents? *(They don't want their parents to become suspicious.)*

6. How does Yingtao feel about not being able to talk to Matthew? *(He is worried about what is going to happen at the recital.)*

7. Why does Yingtao keep looking out the window one hour before the recital is to begin? *(He is looking for a sign from Matthew.)*

8. Why was the Yang family surprised to be served fortune cookies at the restaurant in Chinatown? *(They had not eaten fortune cookies before.)*

9. Why can't Yingtao eat his lunch? *(He is too anxious about Matthew.)*

10. How does Yingtao know his mother is trying to be really nice to him? *(She tells Yingtao that he does not need to finish his rice if he doesn't feel like it. Usually, not finishing food is a bad thing.)*

11. How does Eldest Brother try to encourage Yingtao? *(He tells Yingtao that once he gets the first few measures right, the rest will come easily.)*

12. Why doesn't Third Sister try to cheer up Yingtao? *(She knows how hopeless Yingtao's playing is.)*

13. Why does Yingtao think some of the parents arrive early? *(They are curious to see how a Chinese family lives.)*

14. What kind of sign does Matthew give Yingtao? Why? *(He gives Yingtao the thumbs-up sign; He is trying to tell Yingtao that everything will be fine.)*

15. Why will it be difficult for Matthew to continue playing the violin in the orchestra? *(Girls play most of the string instruments, but boys usually play the wind instruments. The other boys tease Matthew about playing the violin.)*

16. How does Father comfort the girl who loses her place? *(He goes over to her and talks to her for a minute.)*

17. Why does Yingtao worry when he notices the torn place on the screen? *(He is worried that the audience will be able to see Matthew playing the violin.)*

18. Why does Yingtao have a bitter taste in his mouth when he sees his parents smiling at him while the quartet is playing? *(His parents are proud of him for something he didn't do.)*

19. Do you think Third Sister does the right thing by knocking over the screen on purpose? *(Answers will vary.)*

Supplementary Activities

1. Art: Have students draw the scenes Second Sister painted on the screens. This may be an individual or a class project. Display the finished pictures in the classroom.

2. Creative Writing: The Yang family is first introduced to fortune cookies when they eat at a Cantonese restaurant. Have students brainstorm messages that might be found in a fortune cookie. Divide students into groups of three. Have them trade their cookie messages with another group. Each group should read the messages together, then choose one that they think pertains to each individual. Each student should then write a short essay telling why that cookie message is right for him or her. As an alternative, have parents donate money to purchase fortune cookies. Have each student read the message in his/her fortune cookie and tell the class why it does or does not pertain to him/her.

3. Interviewing/Listening: Invite a Chinese American or Chinese immigrant to speak to your class. Instruct students to prepare questions ahead of time that they would like to ask the speaker.

Chapter 7

Vocabulary

frank (115)	torn (117)	dazed (117)	bewildered (119)
trivial (122)	winced (123)	influence (123)	noble (124)
protested (125)	astonished (126)		

Discussion Questions

1. Why do the parents crowd around Mr. Yang after the recital? *(They want to congratulate him on the fine performances.)*

2. Why does Mrs. Schultz ask Second Sister to baby-sit for her? *(Peter, her son, seems to like Second Sister.)*

3. How does Mrs. Yang feel about Second Sister baby-sitting for Mrs. Schultz? *(She wonders why Mrs. Schultz would trust a stranger.)*

4. How does Mrs. Schultz respond to Mrs. Yang's concern? *(She says that Second Sister is not a stranger and she seems to be a serious, responsible girl.)*

5. How do the Conners feel after the recital? *(They are dazed and amazed at Matthew's ability to play the violin.)*

6. What reason does Mrs. Conner give for Mary bumping into the screen? *(She thinks Mary bumped into the screen on purpose so they would know that Matthew was playing the violin.)*

7. Why does Mr. Yang ask, "Who's Mary?" *(Mr. Yang does not know that Third Sister has taken an American name.)*

8. What reason does Mr. Conner give for wanting to pay for Matthew's violin lessons? *(He wants to pay for the lessons because he does not want to accept charity.)*

9. Why does Mrs. Conner say that Yingtao is welcome in their home anytime? *(She believes that Yingtao is a good influence on Matthew.)*

10. Why is Second Sister proud of Yingtao? *(She thinks that Yingtao gave up his place in the quartet so that Matthew could show his father that he is good at playing the violin.)*

11. What does Yingtao think his father is going to tell him? *(Yingtao thinks his father will accuse him of disgracing the family.)*

12. How does Yingtao feel when Mr. Yang tells him that he is proud of him? *(Answers will vary.)*

Supplementary Activities

1. Drama: Have students act out the scene in the recital when Third Sister knocks over the screen and exposes Matthew.

2. Creative Writing: Ask students the following: Think about a time when someone was proud of you for an accomplishment. How did his/her praise make you feel? Write a poem or draw a picture that describes how you felt.

3. Writing: Have students pretend they attended the recital. Instruct them to write a review for a community newspaper about the performance.

Chapter 8

Vocabulary

insisted (127)	wrapped (128)	crimson (128)	persuaded (129)
fingering (129)	scooped (130)	expressionless (130)	soloist (134)
bunt (134)			

Discussion Questions

1. Why does the family stop making Yingtao practice the violin? *(They realize that he does not have a talent for playing the violin.)*

2. Why does Matthew insist upon paying for his violin lessons? *(He wants to feel as if he is doing his share. He does not want charity from Yingtao's father.)*

3. Why does Yingtao loan Matthew his violin? *(Matthew needs a better one to play well.)*

4. How does Yingtao feel about being left out when Matthew plays in the quartet? *(He feels like the blind boy who cannot see the colors of the sunset that are described to him.)*

5. What does Mr. Yang do to show Yingtao that he has forgiven him? *(Mr. Yang gives Yingtao a baseball bat and comes to see him play in a baseball game.)*

6. How does Third Sister encourage the family to attend Yingtao's baseball game? *(She tells her family that Yingtao never complained about practicing the violin or listening to music even though he was bored. The least that they could do is go to his baseball game.)*

7. How does Yingtao feel when he catches the bunt from the other team? *(Answers will vary; Yingtao feels proud that his family sees that he does something well.)*

8. Why does Yingtao think he might never hit a home run? *(Answers will vary.)*

9. Why do Eldest Brother and Second Sister tap the bench with their pencils? *(This is the way that string players tell a soloist or a guest conductor that they think he/she did well.)*

10. Which is better? Having a good ear or having a great eye? *(Answers will vary.)*

Supplementary Activities

1. Critical Thinking: As a class, compare and contrast the way Yingtao feels when he plays baseball to the way he feels when he plays the violin. Have students collaborate on drawing a picture that illustrates how Yingtao and his family feel when Yingtao plays the violin. Have them also draw a second picture illustrating how Yingtao and his family feel when Yingtao plays baseball.

2. Creative Thinking/Writing: Have students write a short story telling what they think the characters from *Yang the Youngest and His Terrible Ear* will do during their summer break from school.

3. Storytelling: Yingtao recalls a Chinese story about a blind boy who cannot see the sunset. Read another Chinese story to the class. Discuss how it is similar/different to other stories students have read.

4. Sports: Organize a baseball or softball game and play as a class, or join with another class. Have students write a short paragraph describing how, based on their own experience, Yingtao must have felt after his big game.

Post-reading Discussion Questions

1. How might things have been different if Matthew had not been Yingtao's friend?

2. What important lessons did Yingtao learn from Matthew? What did Matthew learn from Yingtao?

3. As you read this story, which character did you find most appealing? Why? Which character did you find least appealing? Why?

4. Do you think *Yang the Youngest and His Terrible Ear* is a good title for this book? Why or why not? Make up a new title for the story. Why would this be a good title for the book?

5. Have you read a story similar to this one? What is it? How is it similar? How is it different?

6. If you could change one part of this story, what would it be? Why?

7. If you were part of Yingtao's family, would you want to be a musician? Why or why not?

8. How would the story have been different if it had been told by Matthew? by Second Sister? by Third Sister?

9. Would you recommend this book to a friend? Why or why not?

10. What did you learn from this book? Explain in detail.

11. Why do you think the author wrote this book? Do you think she achieved her goal?

12. Does this story make you feel differently now than you did before reading the book? Why?

13. Discuss an important event in the story. What caused the event? Why do you think this event is important?

14. Describe the main character, Yingtao. Give illustrations of his actions, his conversations, and/or comments by minor characters that help you describe the character.

15. Name other characters that are important to the story. Discuss why these characters are important.

16. Do any of the characters remind you of people you know? In what way?

17. Compare and contrast yourself with Yingtao. In what manner are you like and/or different from Yingtao?

18. What do you think is Yingtao's biggest challenge? Discuss different ways Yingtao could have solved his problems.

19. Do you notice any particular patterns in the form of this novel? Are there any natural breaking points in the story? If so, what are they?

20. Were there any clues built into the story by the author that aided you in anticipating the outcome of the novel? Give examples.

Post-reading Extension Activities

1. Write a short composition explaining how this story can help you in your own life.

2. Imagine that you are one of the main characters and write a diary account of the events of a particular day in the story.

3. Make a collage of the most important events in the novel.

4. If you were to meet Lensey Namioka, the author of *Yang the Youngest and His Terrible Ear*, what questions would you ask her?

5. Make a diorama using a shoebox to depict your favorite scene from the book.

6. Design a different book jacket or poster to advertise the book.

7. Write at least four new titles for the story *Yang the Youngest and His Terrible Ear* that would give the reader an idea of what the book is about.

8. Create stick puppets to reenact a scene from the book.

9. If you could create or change three illustrations from the story, which scenes would you choose? Why? Illustrate one of those scenes and display your drawing in the classroom.

10. Choose a part of the story that you liked very much. Find music that expresses the feeling of the story at that point. Record that section of the story on a tape along with the background music. Add the tape to the classroom listening library.

11. How do the main characters in *Yang the Youngest and His Terrible Ear* change as the story progresses? Why do the characters change? What events contribute to these changes? Choose one character from the book and complete a character chart (see page 26 in this guide) that shows how the character reacts to events in the story and how those events change the character.

12. Write an acrostic poem that describes one of the characters.

    Example: Use parts of speech that describe Yingtao.

    Y - adjective that relates to Yingtao
    I - adverb that relates to Yingtao
    N - verb that relates to Yingtao
    G - adverb that relates to Yingtao
    T - verb that relates to Yingtao
    A - adjective that relates to Yingtao
    O - adjective that relates to Yingtao

13. Design a T-shirt that Yingtao might wear (such as a baseball uniform).

14. Rewrite a section of this story as a comic book.

15. Write a letter to Yingtao and incorporate questions and comments that relate to the story.

16. As a class, design a Web page to advertise this book or other stories about the Yang family.

17. Tell this story in the form of a rap.

18. Create a time line to depict the events in the life of Yingtao.

19. Design a travel brochure about Seattle, Washington. List attractions, rides, and restaurants, particularly those you think Yingtao and his family might enjoy.

20. Write a rhyming poem that describes one of the events in the story. Illustrate this poem.

21. Make a list of traits that Yingtao exhibits in the story. Choose events from the story that support the existence of each trait.

22. Compare and contrast the staple diet of people who live in Shanghai, China to the typical diet of people who live in the Seattle, Washington area. How are they different? How are they similar?

Feelings

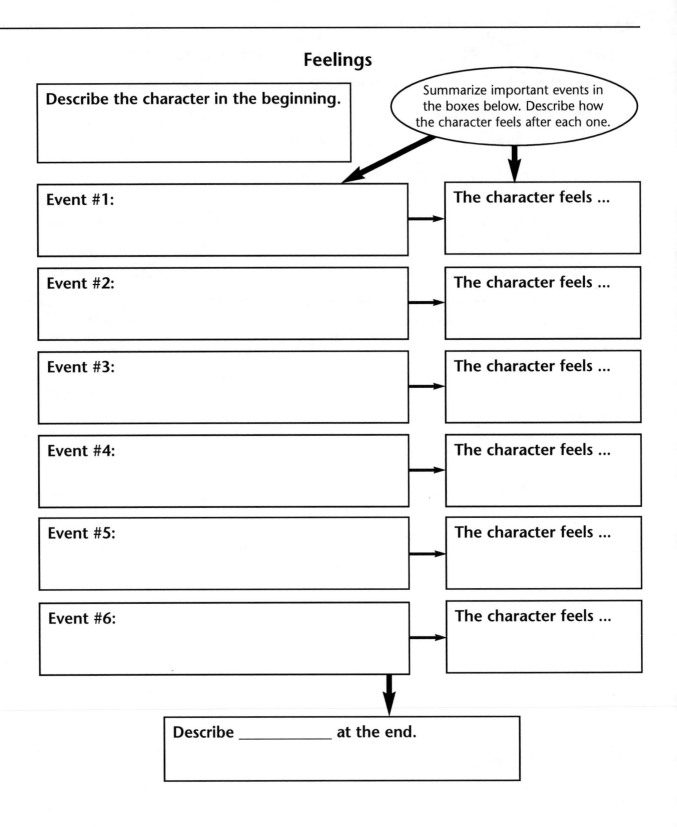

Describe the character in the beginning.

Summarize important events in the boxes below. Describe how the character feels after each one.

Event #1:

The character feels ...

Event #2:

The character feels ...

Event #3:

The character feels ...

Event #4:

The character feels ...

Event #5:

The character feels ...

Event #6:

The character feels ...

Describe _____ at the end.

Assessment for *Yang the Youngest and His Terrible Ear*

Assessment is an ongoing process. The following ten items can be completed during the novel study. Once finished, the student and teacher will check the work. Points may be added to indicate the level of understanding.

Name _____ Date _____

Student   **Teacher**

_____   _____   1. Write a television advertisement and videotape a dramatization of it to encourage another student to read this book.

_____   _____   2. Find five opinion statements and five facts in the story. Rewrite each in your own words.

_____   _____   3. Write a letter to the author of *Yang the Youngest and His Terrible Ear* and tell her how you enjoyed the book.

_____   _____   4. Write a journal entry from another character's point of view (such as Matthew) following the recital.

_____   _____   5. How would the story have ended if Yingtao had actually played in the recital? How would this have affected Matthew, Matthew's parents, the rest of the Yang family, and Yingtao's ability to play baseball? Write a new ending based on these differences.

_____   _____   6. Write a conversation that Yingtao might have with Mr. Yang about baseball.

_____   _____   7. Would you like to have Yingtao as a friend? Why or why not?

_____   _____   8. Find four adjectives and four adverbs in the story that helped create the mood of the story. Use at least two of the adjectives and two of the adverbs in sentences.

_____   _____   9. Rank the main characters in order from best-liked to least-liked.

_____   _____   10. Make a character collage. Cut out words and pictures from magazines that describe one character in the novel. Put the character's name in the collage.

Notes